Let's get this sh!t done!
Potty training made simple.

Table of Contents

Introduction
    What This Book Is About
    What Is Potty Training?
    Why Is Potty Training Important?

Why Do I Need to Teach My Toddler How to Use the Toilet?
    Independence
    Preschool or Daycare Requirement
    Cost of Diapers

Step-By-Step Guide to Successful Potty Training
    Step 1: Introduce the potty and the idea of potty training.
    Step 2: Pick an ideal location and position for the potty.
    Step 3: Dress the toddler in a shirt and "big-kid" underwear.
    Step 4: Give my child plenty of fluids (preferably water).
    Step 5: Take my child to the potty every 20 minutes.
    Step 6: Encourage my child to tell me if they need to use the potty.
    Step 7: Make it a fun experience.

Myths & Misconceptions for Potty Training
    Boys can't be potty-trained as early as girls.
    Beginning early is better because they will learn on their own.
    There's a cut-off age for potty training.
    Daycare centers don't teach potty training.
    That potty-training method will just work!
    Potty training is always a nightmare!

What Are the Methods of Potty Training?
    Elimination Communication Potty Training
    Adult-Lead Potty Training
    Child-Initiated Potty Training
    The Weekend Warrior

What Are the Stages of Potty Training?
    Stage One: Toilet Play
    Stage Two: Toilet Practice
    Stage Three: Toilet Learning
    Stage Four: Independent Toileting

How to Ensure Success with Potty Training

- Make it a positive experience.
- Remain calm (no matter what)!

How is Potty Training Different with Boys Compared with Girls?
- Teach Boys How to Stand Up While Potty Training

What Should I Do Before Starting Potty Training?
- Offer reassurance
- Don't force it
- Consider whether it's the right time
- Don't fight
- Talk about it
- Watch for signs

Potty-Training Tips to Make Toilet Training Easier
- Use books to explain
- Talk about the process
- Show by example
- Encourage potty-training play
- Ask questions
- Don't make it harder

What Should I Do About Regression?
- What Is Regression & How Do I Know If My Child Has It?
  - Changes in diet
  - Illness or food sensitivity
  - Distraction or concentration
  - Stress or life-changing events
- How to Deal with Regression
  - Be patient with support
  - Validate feelings
  - Keep it positive

What Should I Do About Cleanliness With a Toddler?
- How to Teach Wiping
- How to Teach My Child to Clean Up
- How to Prepare for Accidents
  - Think it through
  - Be prepared
  - Avoid jumping to conclusions and blaming
  - Plan better
  - Be understanding
  - How to handle bedwetting
  - Control fluid intake

- Wake them up
- Talk them through it and use nightlights

How to Keep the Potty Chair Clean
- Try a coffee filter
- Use a potty chair liner

How to Clean the Mattress After an Accident
- Blot the urine stain
- Use a vinegar cleaning solution
- Nix the smell of baking soda
- Use a hydrogen peroxide solution

The Takeaway

Introduction

Potty training is one of those times in our lives as parents that we never forget. It can be happy because the kids are moving on with their lives, taking on the next challenge, and developing like they are supposed to. It's also sad. Babies are so much fun, and by the time they get to the toddler stage, they are showing off their personalities. They are full of life and vibrant activities. While potty training is a necessary part of what we teach as parents, it's something that we don't always entirely embrace.

It's not always easy working with our children to achieve potty training success. It's viewed with panic, fear, and terror. Here are just a few reasons to feel that way.

- We don't want to do it because it will take time and energy.
- We're already too busy, and it may just seem more manageable to keep up with the regular diapering schedule.
- It's just not fun, and it can be difficult. But, unfortunately, we cannot finish within a day and then move on to the next stage.

Everyone has a different story about their potty-training adventure. But, I've heard and seen a consistent theme of knowing that it's a necessary evil. Yes, it's something that I knew that I had to take on eventually as a parent. I'd heard other parents talk about it. And, in most cases, those of us who hadn't faced it yet were just hoping that it would be over quickly and easily. But, I always felt I was on the same page, and we were all mutually focused on our kids.

What This Book Is About

This ebook overviews what potty training is, why it's essential, and some reasons you may look for advice. I also talk about some myths and misconceptions about potty training. Many of these myths and misconceptions you may have already heard and wondered about yourself over the years.

I guide you through potty training.

1. I cover the most common methods for potty training and review what the Northern Illinois University Child Develop and Family Center calls the stages of potty training.
2. I cover some tips to ensure success and how potty training may differ for boys and girls.
3. I discuss what to do before starting potty training and how to make it easier and more streamlined.

What Is Potty Training?

Potty training is one milestone in parenting. While potty training may be different for each child, it's simply the process of training a child to use the toilet. IT DIDN'T HAPPEN OVERNIGHT when I taught my kids to use the bathroom. It was a process, but it was such an accomplishment when it was all finished.

Why Is Potty Training Important?

Potty training is essential because it's just part of our focus on a hygienic and healthy lifestyle. Physical or health concerns could mean more prolonged diaper use. Unfortunately, in most cases, I think we take for granted that our kids will just be potty-trained by the time they are 5 or 6 years of age (maybe earlier).

As parents, we play an essential role in how and when potty training starts, and we are also part of the process that ensures that it's over quickly, at least in the best-case scenarios. But, as parents, we can also take a more relaxed approach, letting our children decide how to drive the potty-training practice.

Why Do I Need to Teach My Toddler How to Use the Toilet?

There comes a time in every toddler's life when they need to start to use the toilet instead of continually relying on diapers, pull-ups, or other tools. Of course, a significant part of that progression toward potty training is the cost of diapers and pull-ups, but I had other reasons to teach my toddler how to use the bathroom. And my son had reasons too.

The decision to move forward with potty training is often a collective decision. For us, it was clear when my son was ready to begin. As we progress through this ebook, I'll cover some of the most common signs and signals that indicate when a toddler is ready to start potty training. We'll also discuss the best ways to create and encourage and reward toddlers for working toward a fully diaper-free experience.

While there are some typical ages, I have heard other parents or pediatricians talk about the right time for my child to dive into the potty-training adventure. So, I think we all have to remember not to let the silent judgment or nosy questions of other parents or not-so-well-meaning adults force us to take steps forward when we're not ready. So, here are reasons to start the potty-training adventure.

Independence

Potty training wasn't just a milestone for me. It was a mark that my toddler was growing up and learning to be more independent. Finally, we felt relieved because my child could communicate the need to use the toilet. It was an exciting and rewarding time for my child and me. For him, he felt like he was a "big kid" because he was finally using the toilet "as the big kids do." Unfortunately, while it gave him a feeling of independence, the sheer excitement and novelty of it didn't last for as long as I would have hoped.
Independence is one thing, but the need to stop what he was doing and use the bathroom never held much of an appeal for him. When you're building a tower, or you've got an epic battle going on with dinosaurs, a kid hardly wants to be stalled in his tracks by persistent questioning and reminders, "Let's go use the bathroom, okay?"

Preschool or Daycare Requirement

Of course, independence isn't the only reason to jump into potty training. For many of us parents, it's a requirement or strong suggestion for preschool attendance. So it makes sense that most preschool teachers would prefer a wholly or at least partially potty-trained toddler before making them a part of a structured classroom.

All of that makes sense. So, for me, as a parent, I want to get my kid potty-trained as soon as possible. It opens the possibilities of taking my kid to preschool. It also means that I don't have to pack a bag full of diapers every time I take my kid somewhere, whether it be the babysitter, nanny, or childcare center.

The reason for their potty-training requirement is more than just a nicety. If they have 40+ kids, imagine how much time it would take to change all those diapers? Many childcare workers can change one child's diapers at least five times, even on a good day.

Just imagine what that means when they have 40+ small kids who need regular changes. It's a monumental amount of work to oversee the diaper changes alone. Even with a couple of workers all tasked to manage the kids and, with each diaper change averaging 5-10 minutes each, it's not for the faint of heart.

So, I understand why they want and need the kids to be potty-trained. Even partially potty-trained kids make the daycare worker's life easier. They can do more fun activities with the kids without constantly changing diapers. Also, since daycares often teach socialization skills, it's easier if all the toddlers agree with potty training.

They can watch and learn, even as my childcare worker offers tips and kind suggestions for how to better time those bathroom breaks to avoid accidents. But, of course, the daycare requirement and independence factor are only pieces of the puzzle. Another factor, which is the most important one, involves the cost of diapers.

Cost of Diapers

I've felt the pain of diaper costs even in the best of times. Disposable diapers are a [$71 billion](#) industry, but they take ~500 years for one diaper to decompose. That's why the stinky castoffs stack up in the landfill and always made me wonder how I could deserve to be fated to spend a good part of my paycheck on diapers.

Even in my household trash, those dirty diapers took up as much as 50% of my total household waste every week. With those overwhelming stats, I explored cotton diapers and a range of other options. After all, I could reuse those diapers 50-200 times before they became so tattered that I relegated them to the rag heap.

When I added up the cost of cotton diapers with the cover and all the other niceties, diapers were still not cheap. For the sake of my potty-training discussion, it didn't matter whether I was using disposable or reusable diapers. The disposable diapers were usually more convenient, but I could feel better about my reusable diapers and how they were helping to save the world. Still, either way, it's an additional cost that I incurred as part of parenting.

Every time I bought another pack of diapers or ran another load of diapers through the laundry, it was painful every time. But, when my son was a baby, that pain was easy to overcome. It's just part of being a parent, just like buying or making baby food or any other necessity for the parenting adventures.

For me, there was that defining moment when I realized I needed to take a more proactive approach with my son's potty-training practice. My first step was to do reading and research since that's my preferred approach. I want to know what the experts have to say! So, what do they say about the process of potty training?

Here's a step-by-step overview of the potty-training process. It might be different for each of us, but it's still a great idea to get a sense of the basics and what to expect as we work toward the goal of our children being fully potty-trained.

Step-By-Step Guide to Successful Potty Training

Parenting takes patience. Potty training is one of those processes that will take much longer and require much more patience than we ever knew we could muster. It can be frustrating, and it may even seem downright impossible. But, as we take it one day at a time, we will get through the potty-training process.

Step 1: Introduce the potty and the idea of potty training.

I'd guess that my child knows what the toilet is. It's the fishbowl-looking, splashy place that has tempted them for as long as they can remember. It's also possible, even probably, that you've discovered my child on more than one occasion playing in toilet water. It's gross, and it's often easiest to just hurry them away for a bath, but it's not a foreign concept. Toddlers have been in the bathroom for baths and brushing their teeth every day. Toddlers are notorious for following us into the bathroom as well.

They may understand the general concept, but they may not fully understand how it works or use the toilet or potty seat effectively. So, your task in this first step is to gauge their current level of understanding and then broaden that knowledge base further. With this initial step, invite my child to ask any silly questions that come to mind. For example, my kids loved to watch *Bear in the Big Blue House – Potty Time with Bear*. They also loved *Sesame Street: Elmo's Potty Time* when learning about potty time. There are many options available for books, DVDs, and streaming video. Fun and colorful characters make the idea of potty-time seem accessible and easy to understand.

Of course, that's not the only way to introduce potty time. Our neighbors next door used a "potty" doll. So, her daughter practiced helping the doll use the mini toilet, and my child benefited from watching her play potty training. My son practiced with his stuffed animals, although that can always be something to watch closely to ensure that the toilet is empty when he practices. Then, too, when we used the regular bathroom for potty training, I was always close by to make sure that the favorite stuffed animal or doll didn't fall in.

Step 2: Pick an ideal location and position for the potty.

When my child first started potty training, we used a potty chair. They come in all shapes, colors, and sizes. My kids loved them because they are easy to use, and they are down to their level and size. As a parent, I loved the potty chairs because it theoretically meant that my kid would not fall into the toilet. But unfortunately, there always seems to be at least one incident when a child tries to use the "big" bathroom, and they fall in and make a big splash.

To avoid the potential issue with one or the other scenario, we had a little potty chair they could use whenever they wanted. Then, we had a ladder toilet seat that fits over the regular toilet seat. With the ladder-type toilet seat, we worked together to ensure the experience was as easy as possible since there were always times when my kids needed to use the restroom while shopping or in a restaurant. We also practiced how to use the "big" toilet without the ladder. I made sure that it wasn't a scary experience, no matter where they were or when they used the bathroom.

Step 3: Dress the toddler in a shirt and "big-kid" underwear.

If possible, it's easier to start potty training in the summer. At that time, it's warm enough outside that it's not a big deal for my child to run around in a shirt and underwear/briefs. At this point, the stack of underwear/briefs will have grown. Mainly when we start with potty training, there may be quite a few accidents along the way.

An accident does not usually feel great because it's wet and uncomfortable. It is a beautiful way to encourage them to use the potty chair instead of wetting themselves. They also get a sense of what it feels like when using the potty chair. It's a gradual process of awareness, which leads to more proactive behavior.

Step 4: Give my child plenty of fluids (preferably water).

It might be tempting just to keep the water and other beverages away from a toddler when we're just starting with the potty-training process. Not only is that not safe for a young child, particularly on a hot summer day, but they will still have accidents. It's better and safer to encourage a toddler to drink lots of water.

Hydration and drinking water are part of a healthy lifestyle that will build upon for their entire life. With total hydration, it's also easier for them to get the feeling of having a full bladder and needing to pee. So, once they start understanding what it feels like, our goal is to encourage and support my child in their efforts to use the bathroom.

Yes, it could be a hassle at the store when my child needs to use the bathroom every 5 minutes. It may also be outside the realm of easy logistics. It's okay to rely on a pull-up to get through those times, especially during those first stages of the potty-training process.

The same is true if you're traveling. I've missed flights when one of my kids needed to use the bathroom right as we were boarding. Unfortunately, they may not get to a restroom right away in all buildings or locations, so we all need to plan and figure out how to best handle the situation.

Step 5: Take my child to the potty every 20 minutes.

With each of these steps, we are better at building practices that will be easier to manage as time goes on. At first, I started taking my son to use the potty chair every 20 minutes. Even if he didn't feel like he needed to use the bathroom, I still asked him to try. Then, as my son learned to fully understand what it feels like when they have the urge to pee, we didn't need to make the trip quite as often. It stretched out to every 30 minutes and then more prolonged and extended until he learned to go when the urge was there. Here's a quick, easy-to-follow schedule:

- Each morning when they first wake up
- Right after the mid-morning snack
- Before the nap time

- After waking up from the nap
- Before starting the bedtime routine at night

With the regular repetition and habit of using the bathroom regularly, I gradually proved the importance of that consistency in the scheduled frequency. It quickly becomes apparent that life is easier and more fun without diapers.

Step 6: Encourage my child to tell me if they need to use the potty.

The first steps of potty training involve lots of hands-on attention, coaxing, encouraging words, and reminding about using the toilet. Fortunately, there comes a time when that level of hands-on intervention is not needed, at least not to the same extent.

So, the next step is the process of empowerment. They may not fully articulate what they want when they are 18 months or even two years old, but I encourage them to express their needs and desires. For example, when do they need to use the bathroom? What does it feel like? What else do they need?

Beyond asking questions and validating their feelings and thoughts about potty training, it's essential to encourage them to express their fears, doubts, concerns, and ideas. Sometimes that can get wild when their imaginations start going, but this is a perfect time to begin to connect.

Demonstrate how and why their potty-training experience is so important. Make sure they feel heard and understood, no matter how silly their ideas or thoughts may be. By the time they get to preschool or kindergarten, their exploration of poop jokes will be discouraged. So, allow them the safe space to figure out what is so fascinating about bodily functions in a safe and non-judgmental space.

Step 7: Make it a fun experience.

With all those poop jokes, silly stories, and drawings, I think most parents may feel like they've maxed out on all the poop-tastic talk that one person can handle. It's okay. It may not be easy to remember, but it's possible that all of us were the same way when we were toddlers. So be open to the experience of talking about poop. It's a normal part of life, and it will be something our kids will deal with for the rest of their life.

One constant in my life is change and growth. Just because they're fascinated by poop and everything to do with bodily functions today doesn't mean that fascination won't change tomorrow. If I want to have some fun, I can watch documentaries on dung beetles on Prime's Curiosity Stream or explore bugs galore on Discovery+.

Curiosity and a love for knowledge are remarkable things for us to encourage in our kids, even if it can be slightly embarrassing when they blurt out something about poop in the checkout line at the grocery store. I could wish the floor would just open up and swallow me whole as shoppers and workers alike turn to stare at you. Or, I could just say, "That's a great thought! What do you think?" So, let's dig in on some tried-and-true potty training methods. Here's what we all should know.

Myths & Misconceptions for Potty Training

Potty-training experiences are different for every child and every family situation. There's no one way to do it, but everyone will offer sage wisdom and advice on which method is best. Unfortunately, while I've heard lots of great advice and tips over the years, I've also heard many myths and misconceptions about potty training.

Many of these fictions are based on parents' beliefs and understanding about their children. Often, they've heard all sorts of stories that may just make the process scarier than it ever needs to be. Here are just a few examples:

Boys can't be potty-trained as early as girls.

The myth about boys vs. girls and how soon they can be potty-trained is one of the most often repeated myths and misconceptions. While boys may take a different approach and more preparation, boys and girls can participate in potty training if they are interested and ready to begin.

In addition, anatomical differences between boys and girls may prompt us to teach our sons to sit down while peeing and pooping. But, starting in a seated position, it's just simplifying the process. So, my son could learn the basics of potty training without needing to have the aim and trajectory down yet.

Beginning early is better because they will learn on their own.

I've heard parents say that it's important to start potty training before my child is 2 years old. For some kids, that might work great if they are ready to start. However, for my kids and for other kids that I've cared for and known, they just weren't prepared that early, and we never pressured them to try potty training before they were prepared. Some parents also heard that their children started early and just learned independently.

Kids can figure out all kinds of behaviors, and potty training could very well be one of those things our kids can just figure out. However, I'd hesitate to suggest that figuring it out on their own is typical for most kids, and there's nothing wrong with a child who still wears a diaper at 2 years old. If you're concerned about your child's development, I always ask our pediatrician and nurse practitioner. They had such great advice and tips, based on how my kids were progressing.

There's a cut-off age for potty training.

Potty training is a developmental milestone, which means that not all kids will be ready at the same age. Each child may develop at slightly different rates and speeds, like walking or talking. Developmental milestones and readiness are both topics that we as parents can and will discuss with our pediatrician or nurse practitioner as we watch for signs of body awareness and self-care abilities. It's not a topic to avoid or feel that it's taboo.

Instead, talking about potty training and figuring out the best ways to help our kids through it is just a part of life, which does not mean that it will happen at any date, time, or age. However, there are great resources: books, doctors, nurses, and friends. Take advantage of them to figure out the best time for my child.

Daycare centers don't teach potty training.

Indeed, daycare centers and preschools usually prefer incoming children to be at least partially potty trained for specific ages, usually in the range of 3 or 4 years old. A few of the stricter daycare centers require that they be "potty trained," but the definition itself is debatable. Many of the kids in a part-or-full-time daycare situation will have accidents, at least occasionally. Some parents prefer to place their kids in a flexible potty-training policy program because the peer pressure of watching other kids use the bathroom regularly can sometimes help in the training. But, of course, they want to do that too!

That potty-training method will just work!

Some parents believe that using one potty-training method will work, even when all others have failed. There's a reason there are so many methods out there. Not every potty-training method will work for every child. I may have even tried every single one of them without success, and that's okay. It doesn't mean you've done anything wrong or that there's anything wrong with the potty-training methods. It just means that the way(s) we've tried didn't work right now for my child. It may be that we could try the same approach in six months, and you'll sail through the process with no issues at all. It could be that my child was already familiar with the potty-training method. Or they may not be ready!

Potty training is always a nightmare!

That's probably the biggest myth and misconception of all. Potty training can have moments of frustration and struggle, but it's also a time of growth, learning, and celebration. Even when there are hard days, with lots of accidents, it's all part of the process. It rarely happens overnight, but it happens eventually. And, oh, what a celebration that is!

What Are the Methods of Potty Training?

While many of us don't use just one method with our potty training, some helpful strategies are. Here are four main ways I explored when potty training my children. Most of us examine a few different techniques to determine which one is the most effective for our child. We found the potty-training method that worked for us, and I hope you'll find one that works for you.

Here are a few options.

Elimination Communication Potty Training

If you're looking to start potty training at the earliest possible moment, elimination communication might work for you. It involves watching for critical signals that show that my child is ready to begin potty training. It's tied into attachment parenting theories, and the practice can start as early as birth, but it's more typical up to four months old.

If I want to try it, it's simple. When I started to see the signals that my child was ready to poop or pee, I just put my baby on a potty chair or even a regular toilet seat in the bathroom. It can be challenging to start because infants are not always very talkative. Or their talk may be "baby talk," which may be cute but may not be as articulate or informative as we'd like. So, it's more about recognizing what different cries mean and learning to read their body language.

While some parents swear by it, I never used the method extensively. For one, it's time-consuming to scoop them up and run them to the toilet or potty chair every five minutes. There are a few positive side effects, though. When I'd run him to the potty chair every time there was the slightest indication that he had to relieve himself, I did use fewer diapers.

With this method, parents say that it streamlines the entire potty-training process. With elimination communication, my child was starting to get a sense of what we were trying to do. Of course, he thought it was hilarious, but for those parents who keep it up, there will be widespread benefits and less work when the real work of potty training begins.

To me, though, even though it still sounds too good to be true. Yes, it sounds great to think that I could start ending your reliance on diapers at 4 months of age. But some pediatricians say that a child isn't even ready to start potty training until they are 18 months (about 1 and a half years) old. Still, if it works for you, why not do it?

If there's no pressure on my child to be instantly potty-trained, it will be an excellent exercise for you, and you'll get to spend lots of quality time with my child running back and forth to the bathroom. It's not hurting anyone, so try it out and see if it works. Then, at least consider some other methods for potty training.

Adult-Lead Potty Training

I helped my toddler use the toilet or potty chair in adult-lead potty training. We continued to use diapers and pull-ups, but we focused on sticking to our potty schedule. Since we still used diapers, it wasn't a big deal if there was an accident in between potty breaks, but it was a great way to get my son used to the idea of using the toilet.

With this method, I needed to keep on a tight schedule, and I always needed to make sure that his babysitter or nanny was also consistent with his plan. It was never the end of the world when I used diapers as interludes between the regularly scheduled bathroom visits. The entire process was still within our control.

Of course, it was always more manageable if we were both home and other adults were around to help with keeping us on schedule. So, beyond the great consistency we get from following a regular plan with potty training, I prepared him for preschool and eventually kindergarten.

As kids get older, your whole family will have more demands on their time, with strict adherence to schedules and requirements, particularly in classroom settings. So, the sooner they get used to the schedule-focused days, the easier it becomes. But kids also really like a sense of consistency, so they know what to expect, where they will be, what they will do when they eat or drink, and all the rest.

Child-Initiated Potty Training

It's not always easy to communicate with a child when they are so young. A child-initiated approach allows my child to decide the best time. In this scenario, it's best if there's no real rush to finish the potty-training process. In other words, your preschool, regular outings, or other critical events or activities are not pending.

While it may not have as much oversight as the adult-initiated version, it's great to feel like my child can figure out when he is ready physically, mentally, and emotionally. It could happen somewhere in the 2- or 3-years-old age range, or it could happen older. Since you're not in a rush, you're not putting undue stress on my child to grow up and use a toilet.

Of course, it means that you'll be using diapers or at least pull-ups for a longer time, and it may mean more limited childcare options in the short term. But it's incredible how much that superficial level of acceptance allows us to go with the flow and not fight or stress over potty training. It will happen someday, but not until my child is ready.

Even though it is still child-focused, that doesn't mean that we can't talk about the potty, ask about their feelings, and gauge their perceptions on the entire process. Even when you're not pushing, I've seen instances where kids suddenly decided that it was time, and they instantly became potty proficient.

It's just a different process for each kid, so even though it may not always make sense to us, as parents, it makes sense to them. And it's worth exploring whether it's worthwhile just letting my child drive his potty-training effort. Since each kid is so different, I discovered they need a better understanding of what it feels like to need a potty break, but we can also work through the challenges and drawbacks as we go along. There's no one way that's right or wrong to continue in this potty-training adventure.

The Weekend Warrior

When my child was ready for potty training, it was a quick and easy process. With this method, the premise is that we can take a 3-day weekend to process the potty training. It's the perfect way to complete the potty-training process when starting school or preschool.

Weekend Warrior could even be a good possibility for children 22+ months of age who are just ready to flip the switch to be fully potty-trained. It's an expedited process. So, we can throw all your diapers away on the first day. Then, we just follow the strategies that you've already explored with other potty-training methods.

Even if (or when) my child has an accident, I can scoop them up and let them finish on the potty chair or toilet. The goal is to help my child understand how and why potty training is necessary. Then, you'll explain the importance of using the potty chair and help them identify what that urge to go feels like.

THERE WILL BE MANY ACCIDENTS when I use the Weekend Warrior potty training approach, but that's okay. My focus is on making it a safe space to figure it out and explore the potty-training process. All that practice leads to improvements. So, your toddler is potty-trained by the end of the three days. That doesn't mean, of course, that they will have no further accidents. But they've achieved a healthy balance.

What Are the Stages of Potty Training?

According to [Northern Illinois University Child Develop and Family Center](#), there are four main stages of potty training. So, let's go through the essential stages to explore what that means for potty training.

Stage One: Toilet Play

The first step for most children is to conduct toilet play. It starts with an interest in potty training. My child asked lots of questions about bathroom behaviors. Next, they might pretend to use the restroom, even with their clothes on. My child could pretend to potty-train with dolls, toys, or stuffed animals.

Stage Two: Toilet Practice

The next stage in potty training is all about practice. First, I showed my child how to flush, and then they practiced flushing *a lot*. My goal was to help my child practice getting ready to use the potty by encouraging them to start becoming more participatory in their dressing in the morning and undressing at night. I also made it fun to sit on the toilet or potty seat and get up.

Get into the practice of asking: "Are you wet or dry?" Be careful about the language we use because it will make a difference in how my child perceives the potty-training practice. While we have already practiced washing hands, now is another critical opportunity to step the training up to the next level. It's even more important for my child to wash his hands thoroughly to prevent the spread of disease, to prevent illness, and just to support a healthy lifestyle.

Stage Three: Toilet Learning

Beyond the play and the practice, the next stage is learning what that "gotta go" feels like. Some kids use hand gestures, but I could usually tell they were ready based on facial expressions. In addition to having those cues, my kids also needed to know how to "hold it" for more extended periods.

Part of this learning process involves an interest in "real" underwear, a desire to be clean and dry, and the ability to use the bathroom with some degree of independence or self-advocacy. For example, my child could sit and stand, but he also needed to figure out when they were wet and let me know they needed to be changed. It was also vital that they could concentrate on the task.

Stage Four: Independent Toileting

For this stage, it's all about encouraging my child to make the potty-training process their own, with their favorite underwear to make the process feel more personal. All the character-focused underwear helps my child to feel special, like a "big kid," and it's also a reward for their potty-training focus. It could be Barbie, Marvel superheroes, or even Star Wars.

All your focus at this stage is on offering positive reinforcement and encouragement. If they have a tough time going, I can turn on the water in the sink even when they feel the urge. Let my child be in charge as much as possible. Potty training is about preparing myself and my child to take control of the situation.

To best prepare them for potty training, use proper vocabulary. In addition, read books about potty training for parents and potty training for kids. It helps to normalize the potty-training process, makes them feel they are not alone in their struggles, and may even help them relax and feel more comfortable with the entire process.

As part of the effort to encourage independence, offer multiple options for potty training with a potty chair, potty ladder, or step stool. During the process with my son, we talked with him regularly, checking in to see how he was doing if there was anything we could do to make the process easier or more comfortable.

This is a significant milestone for kids, but it also doesn't have to be scary or uncomfortable. Beyond using books as an educational tool, I can also give my child a book or kids' magazine to read while sitting on the toilet or potty chair. Having something to read helps my child relax and take their time through the potty-training process. If my child does feel uncomfortable or embarrassed about the process, it's time to find ways to help alleviate that discomfort. Even when they are still toddlers, what they hear from friends or overhear from adults can distress them and cause them to jump to all the wrong conclusions.

Be sure to use positive reinforcement and language like: "Good job" or "That's awesome!" or "You did it." We always tried to make the process as encouraging and positive as possible. It's not a rush kind of scenario. We could make sure that every part of the potty-training process is understandable by taking time.

How to Ensure Success with Potty Training

Whether I use a rewards system or verbal praise and encouragement, remember to highlight the progress made and the next milestone in the potty-training journey. It's not a big deal when there are accidents. They are standard parts of life and easily remedied. Here are some tips to get started.

Use easy-to-change clothing, particularly in the initial learning process. Clothes that are hard to remove, like overalls, onesies, or dresses, make the potty-training process overly complicated. Ensure that my child knows how to remove their clothes before trying them alone in a bathroom.

Make it a positive experience.

Potty training should be about positive reinforcement, not threats, embarrassment, or punishments. Don't force my child to stay in the bathroom "just in case." It can reinforce scary vibes and misconceptions for kids. Make sure my child is ready before starting the potty-training process. Starting too soon just starts everyone off on the wrong foot.

Remain calm (no matter what)!

Be calm and collected about the process. Your stress levels will make the situation more stressful and upsetting for my child. Avoid comparisons between your kids, friends, or any other child. Every kid is different, and they will move forward and succeed at their own pace and time. Nothing worth doing ever happens overnight. Take time and support their needs to have the best possible experience.

How is Potty Training Different with Boys Compared with Girls?

Potty training doesn't necessarily have to be easier for your daughter than your son, but most parenting experts say that girls tend to ditch diapers faster than boys. Girls may start as early as 22-30 months on average, while boys may take up to 6 months longer to start their potty training. However, studies show that boys and girls are often ready around the same age, sometime between 1 1/2 years (or 18 months) and 2 1/2 years (or 30 months), but boys may not be trained until 31 months compared to girls' 29 months.

It's difficult to gauge whether that general difference in the potty training has more to do with my child's comfort, a parent's insistence, differing comfort levels, or what the variables may be. If a boy had the desire to start potty training, there's every reason to believe that he'd be able to accomplish it, particularly with support from his parents and caregivers. The same is valid for girls. So, while these general statistics are helpful as we plan to start potty training my child, it's complicated.

Teach Boys How to Stand Up While Potty Training

Even as my son discovered the joys of potty training, the question of when to teach him how to "stand and pee" is a frequent question. Other moms have asked me, and I indeed asked how they handled it. So the question we may be asking is not really about whether they are ready, but rather a matter of how much of a mess we want to deal with as they learn how to get it right.

Anatomical differences mean that boys just pee differently, so they need to learn to gently push their penis down when they aim at the toilet bowl or potty chair. For that matter, a boy needs a certain level of control and the ability to aim at least in the right general direction. If there's a dad or male figure in the home, the easy solution is to have him take care of it. "Go show him how to do it!"

I know more than a few moms have said that to their husbands or significant others. But unfortunately, even when a dad does show the boy how to pee standing up, the toddler may not get the timing and aim quite right for some time, often not until he's at least 3 years old. With that much of a delay, it can be frustrating for parents.

What Should I Do Before Starting Potty Training?

Stressful situations can make the process of potty training that much more complicated and complex, which is why it's essential to consider transitional states as part of your decision of when to start potty training.

- You're moving to a new house, or my child moves from their crib to the big-kid bed.
- It could be that there's a new baby in the family.
- A relative might be visiting, which could be enormously stressful.
- Another scenario could involve visiting a family member or friends for a prolonged period.

While any of these factors could make it seem like the best time to start potty training, the stress, uncertainty, and personal fear can lead to an impossible situation. So, if you're wondering why potty training isn't working, take a giant step back and look at some reasons my child could be stressed and thus not as receptive to your efforts to start the potty-training process.

Offer reassurance

Before jumping in, it's in your best interests to let things settle down and reassure my child that I don't expect anything from them during this stressful period. Then, when time has passed, and my child seems more open and receptive to the idea of potty training, give it another shot.

Don't force it

None of us succeed very well if we force it. All you'll manage to do is make my child more uncertain about themselves, their abilities, and even their future. I want to set my child up for success, no matter how long I must wait or what I need to do to reassure and bring comfort to him during a challenging time.

Consider whether it's the right time

Even if stress isn't the issue, we should look at how old my child is and whether it's just too soon. As we study the issues surrounding your potty-training efforts, remember that if we start too early, we may just leave our kids confused, fearful, angst-ridden, and hesitant to do anything related to potty training.

Don't fight

Particularly with a stubborn child, why fight a battle that's not even winnable? Some moments are frustrating, but I do not take a considerable step back or drop it altogether. Instead, put the potty chair in the garage and let it gather dust for a bit. It will still wait there when I need it again. It's also the opportunity for my toddler to use it in play scenarios. That's a good thing!

Talk about it

Get back to talking about the potty-training terminology. I encouraged my child to play with the potty chair and just monitor how he was coping with the stresses and upheavals in life. We've all had them, so why is it so shocking that it might affect our toddlers too?

Once they're fully invested in the potty-training process, and when they're getting those signals from their bladder that it's full (and not ignoring them), it might be time to start again at the beginning of the process. But it may just take them a little longer to recognize those signals for what they were or to respond to the call of the potty chair.

Watch for signs

For my kids, one signal that they were finally getting ready was when they would disappear when they had to go poo in their diaper. While it's nice to hear the advice and tips from other moms, doctors, nurses, and every stranger on the street, I listened to my child and was not afraid to stop the potty-training process when it was overwhelming.

I avoided as much trauma, fighting, and frustrations as possible by taking my time with the potty-training process. So, my recommendation to parents is: "Don't force it!" When my kids were ready, it was amazing how quick and easy it could be!

Potty-Training Tips to Make Toilet Training Easier

When I buy a potty, I put it in the bathroom and explain to my child that it's for them. Go more profound than that, though. Explain how the potty chair works, how we will clean it, and where to keep it. At first, it might just be a novelty item at first, but the more my child uses it, the more they will become comfortable with it.

Use books to explain

Use books to explain the potty-training process. With the myriad of options available, we can easily find books that focus on the topics that concern my child. Then, as we read the books to my child, it should help improve their sense of safety and confidence in their abilities and in your willingness to support them in this potty-training effort.

Talk about the process

While explaining the entire process to my child is essential, a schedule makes life easier. At first, it's a matter of taking my child to sit on the toilet or potty chair for short periods to get them used to the idea. Then, while they are on the toilet, you can also sit on the regular toilet, with your clothes still on, to demonstrate how normal and easy it is.

Show by example

It's also likely that my child will want to emulate your actions and behavior, so it makes the entire process less scary. If we read to them, listen to music, or work on other fun activities to pass the time, we can further reinforce the safe and secure vibe of your potty-training demo.

Encourage potty-training play

Encourage my child to play-act to see how dolls, stuffed animals, and action figures might use the (clean) potty chair for various reasons. Also, use their favorite toys to allow them to understand the potty-training process better. They can explain how to use the potty, what it's for, and they can even read the books to their favorite stuffed pals.

Ask questions

We can ask questions about their feelings throughout the day and find out when they need to go pee or poop. They may not make it every time, but it's also a way to get them closer to understanding the sensations and what their body tells them.

Don't make it harder

The potty-training process doesn't have to be complicated, complex, or impossible. Instead, it should be an easy-to-understand process that helps my child better understand their own needs and desires and what they'll do to recognize what's going on. Then, they'll be ready for whatever new feelings and sensations they experience with positive reinforcement.

What Should I Do About Regression?

Potty training is complicated, and it's not always as smooth sailing as you'd like it to be. Accidents happen. Often there's an accident now and then when my child's timing isn't quite right or when other factors delay access to a bathroom. However, when accidents continue to happen over time, we should consult with your pediatrician to see if a medically related issue may be involved.

While it's essential to check in with your doctor just to make sure you're not overlooking anything more serious, it's still likely that the cause for the ongoing accidents is regression, which can be triggered by environmental or emotional reasons.

What Is Regression & How Do I Know If My Child Has It?

Potty training regression usually refers to a series of accidents that happen after my child appears to be potty-trained. My kids faced regression, including accidents and sudden neglect of potty-training habits. First, we looked at the potential causes to see if something stood out. Of course, it was different for each child. Let's look at what some of those causes may be. Here are some common reasons for regression:

Changes in diet

Maybe they are now attending preschool or daycare, going over to friends' houses, or even spending time with grandparents. So, they are trying new foods and drinking different beverages. There's absolutely nothing wrong with having new experiences with food.

It just means that we need to counteract the effects of those new experiences with probiotics, more fruits and veggies, and more water. In addition, a change in their regular diet can cause constipation (hard stools) or stomach discomfort, which may mean they might avoid using the toilet or potty chair.

Illness or food sensitivity

Kids stop using the bathroom for lots of reasons. First, it could just be that the accident is because they are not feeling well. If it's a stomach issue, it could be something to do with an intestinal bug, food poisoning, or even food sensitivity. If they have a urinary tract infection or constipation, they could avoid the discomfort associated with peeing or pooping.

So, they could have a good reason for their regression. If a child cries when we urge them to use the bathroom or if certain foods seem to directly correlate to their reversal or avoidance of the toilet, listen and act by talking to your pediatrician.

Distraction or concentration

Yep, it could be a distraction! When my kids focused on doing something, whether eating, watching TV, or even playing outside, they hated to stop for a potty break. It took precious moments away from what they were doing, so they often waited until it was too late.

While It's not fun to deal with an accident, it's understandable. It's something that we as adults do as well. The difference is that we tend to have larger bladders and the ability to tell when we just can't wait any longer.

Stress or life-changing events

Stress does affect our toddlers just like it affects our older kids. When the kids are 2 or 3 years old, they just might not have a way to express their feelings. Maybe you're moving or renovating the house, starting a new job, or returning to the old one. Even if we think it's a secret, things like divorce, changes in relationships, or other life-changing events can affect them too.

For them, it could also involve starting a new preschool, finding out they will soon have a new sibling or any myriad of other events in their lives. Our toddlers may not sit down and tell us how they are feeling, but it may just come out with regression when they refuse to use the toilet, seem to forget, or just seem unmotivated.

How to Deal with Regression

By now, I've talked about some of the most common reasons that kids may experience regression issues. It could be something stressing them out, or it could be a health or medical issue. Whatever the reason for their bathroom avoidance or regression, we can work through it and help my child to feel more confident about the entire potty-training process.

Be patient with support

It's not an easy time in a toddler's life, and potty training may just be too much to manage right now. So, don't look at it as a failure. Take a step back and try a different approach to potty training.

When I felt particularly frustrated, I reached out for some fellow-parent support. I was often surprised by how similar your experience was. We all need help to be patient with our kids as they go through this.

Validate feelings

Yes, confirm feelings, but we should allow ourselves to feel them. Validation means that we listen and acknowledge those feelings. Next, act on that knowledge. Finally, if external forces affect the regression, find ways to address those issues by talking about them and working.

Keep it positive

It's easy to get frustrated, mainly when you'd thought that potty training was all done. More than anything, it's essential to stay positive and focus on getting through it together. Freaking out and yelling only makes matters worse and may cause further regression and withdrawal. When we remain calm and collected, we can better strategize addressing the regressive tendencies. It's also a fantastic way to work through the causes triggering the regression. Then, we may find that you're happy and healthier together as we cope with the issues.

What Should I Do About Cleanliness With a Toddler?

Cleanliness is a great goal, but it may be a bit much to expect your toddler to clean themselves when they use the portable potty chair or the toilet. So while it's important to teach them the importance of keeping the bathroom clean and sanitized, I found it more productive to ask my toddler to come and get me when he was done.

Accidents sometimes just happen. There doesn't even always have to be a real reason. Most children enjoy playing, and just a few minutes of extra time spent building a tower or playing in the sand is just enough time for an accident to happen. So instead of blaming, move forward with what we can do next time. Keep the potty chair (or toilet) clean. While my child must learn the fundamentals of the potty-training process, they also need to know about good personal hygiene.

How to Teach Wiping

As they learn how to wipe and take responsibility for their care and cleaning, they need to know how to properly wipe themselves, wash their hands, and properly take care of clothing when they are wet or dirty. But unfortunately, recent studies have shown that many Americans simply don't know how to wipe correctly, from front to back.

So, they could be causing irritation and infection, particularly if they are not taking the time to do it properly. It might seem a lofty goal to teach toddlers to put their wet and dirty clothes in the laundry, but it is possible.

How to Teach My Child to Clean Up

And, even when they forget, a gentle reminder usually sets them back on track. The main thing with teaching my kids how to clean and properly dispose of clothing in the laundry is to make sure that they don't sit around all day in wet and dirty clothes.

How to Prepare for Accidents

It would be nice to think that I'll be standing by in the wings to take care of all these issues for them, and I usually have been. When they are at preschool, daycare, or even kindergarten, a dry change of clothes that they can slip into by themselves can do wonders for the worst possible day for most toddlers I know.

Think it through

When I think and plan about when and where accidents might occur, it is easier to be prepared, right? So, take some time and think about it. It could happen when you're at the store, preschool, when you're heading out the door, at your friend's house, or even at the park. Think about what we would have and what we would do if the situation were ideal and well-planned-out.

Be prepared

When you've thought it through, you've already figured out that we need to stash or bring changes of clothes to prepare for future accidents or other emergencies. However, just because my child isn't in diapers doesn't mean we should leave the "go bag" at home.

Instead of diapers, include a change of clothes, a plastic bag for wet clothes, hand sanitizer, and water. I always had snacks, as well, because we never know when we might need a snack to distract the kid while you're cleaning them up. The snack also helps put them on a more even-keel if the accident is stress-related.

Avoid jumping to conclusions and blaming

Accidents sometimes just happen. There doesn't even always have to be a real reason. Most children enjoy playing, and just a few minutes of extra time spent building a tower or playing in the sand is just enough time for an accident to happen. So instead of blaming, move forward with what we can do next time.

Plan better

Keep track of where the bathroom is at the park (if there is one), or plan to take a potty break before going to the park. Then, help my child change into clean, dry clothes and move forward with your activities. Again, don't link it with fault, but it is an opportunity to be better prepared in the future.

Just because we didn't think it would happen doesn't mean it won't happen. Often there may be situations where an activity or event took longer than expected. For example, we didn't plan for the long line in the bathroom, or we thought there'd be a bathroom facility to use. All those reasons are valid and reasonable. However, it still happened, and now we know for next time.

Be understanding

We should remind ourselves and our kids that it's all-new through this entire process. It's different, and we won't get it right the first time. We're all works in progress. So it's okay to step back occasionally to make sure we've got the whole potty-training thing down, but also understand that your situation is evolving.

Just because it's worked so far doesn't mean we won't need to figure out new ways to handle the evolving potty-training situations as we go along. Will there be unforeseen circumstances? Yes! Will there be explosive diarrhea? Almost, certainly. Will we get through all those accidents and explosive events? Yep, we will.

How to handle bedwetting

Bedwetting is not unusual. 1-in-6 kids (7 million kids) around the ages of 3-12 wet their bets. It's more common in boys than girls, but 20% of US kids are still bedwetting at age, and the numbers decrease from there. Only about 1-3% of kids wet their bed by the time they are teenagers.

Control fluid intake

A great way to avoid issues with bedwetting is to encourage them to drink water earlier in the evening. But keep in mind a "cut-off" time when you'll minimize fluid intake. In addition, enabling water intake earlier in the evening helps them understand the direct correlation between drinking water and the need to use the bathroom.

Wake them up

The real issue for some kids is that they are just so sound asleep that they can't wake up when they need to use the bathroom at night. To help them with that issue, we can wake them up before bed. If that's still too early, gauge when the accidents most often happen and wake them up just before that time. For example, if my son had accidents around 2 am, I could wake him an hour or two before that time to avoid bedwetting.

Talk them through it and use nightlights

Some toddlers and even older kids refuse to get out of bed at night because they are afraid of the dark. Or they may be nervous that there are monsters under the bed or hiding in the shadows. This issue can be worse if they've just watched a scary movie, but it could happen at any time. Any time they seem hesitant to walk to the bathroom, try these tips:

- Encourage them to talk about why the dark appears scary.
- Explain to them that you'll always be there to help them get through it.
- Place nightlights in their room, in the hallway, and the bathroom.
- Talk about monsters and find out what may have triggered their fear.

Once we understand more about the cause of their regression, we can work to help our children overcome their fear. Remind them and yourself that these fears and concerns are common for kids, particularly at stressful times in their lives. It's okay to feel scared, but it's also an opportunity to strategize overcoming that fear.

How to Keep the Potty Chair Clean

The idea of having a potty chair that's the perfect size for your toddler was a great idea in theory, but that also means that we need to keep it clean and sanitized. Yep, there's just one more thing to clean in an already toddler, topsy-turvey house. It's not as hard as it looks, though. Here are a few tips:

Try a coffee filter

Use your paper coffee basket filter for the bowl part of the potty chair. Think of it as the wax paper on a cookie sheet. It keeps the poop from sticking to the bottom and sides, and that's what makes the potty chair frustrating to clean.

Don't let the potty chair sit long between uses without cleaning it out, even with your trusty filter fix. Jump on it, and just throw the coffee filter and poop into the outside trash. Like most things, don't flush it down the toilet or rinse it down the sink. Clean and disinfect your potty chair before subsequent use.

Use a potty chair liner

Yes, they have liners explicitly made for potty chairs. We can find them with a quick search of Amazon or a visit to Target. Unfortunately, the cost for the specially made liners tends to be a bit more than a coffee filter, but they are also more like tiny plastic bags.

With the potty chair liner, I would just make sure that it's the right fit for my potty chair. When my toddler used the potty chair, it poured the urine in the toilet and then tied off the bag like we would with a regular trash bag. Then, we just disinfect the potty chair so it's ready for use.

How to Clean the Mattress After an Accident

When my child has a bedwetting incident, the first step is to strip the bed. Then, put the sheets and blankets in the laundry. But there's more to the accident than the sheets and blankets on the bed or crib. So, how do we clean the stain and prevent it from getting wet and stained next time? Here's how to clean the mattress after a bedwetting accident:

Blot the urine stain

First, blot the spot. Then, repeatedly press down with a towel to soak up the urine. We can also use a wet vac to remove the moisture from the mattress.

Use a vinegar cleaning solution

Use a 50/50 concoction of white vinegar and warm water in a spray bottle to apply to the mattress, and then blot it again with a towel. We might need to air out the room by opening the window or using a fan to eliminate the vinegar smell.

Nix the smell of baking soda

You can neutralize the smell by sprinkling baking soda on the spot. Let it dry for ~10 hours, then vacuum the baking soda.

Use a hydrogen peroxide solution

For more severe stains, use a mixture of 8 ounces of hydrogen peroxide and 3 tablespoons of baking soda. Then, add 2-3 drops of dishwashing liquid. Spray the cleaning solution onto the mattress. Let the solution dry, and vacuum it off.

We can use many cleaning solutions to blot out the urine and cover up the smell. Of course, we can also use a waterproof mattress mat or cover to prevent the stain from reaching the mattress. We can also use pull-ups, nighttime underwear, or even disposable bed underpads to protect your mattress and keep it dry.

The Takeaway

Potty training isn't rocket science, but it involves many variables that might make it challenging to succeed the first time we try. We still have more time, and we're all still learning as we go along which methods will work best for our children. I hope my potty-training tips help you with your child. I'd love to be a part of reassuring you that potty training is not as complex as you may have thought. Potty training takes time, effort, and patience. But it should be fun. Who wants to make it more torturous than it has to be?

Mostly potty training comes down to readiness and parents' encouragement. Of course, there will be accidents, and we may have to try several methods. You'll find what works best for you. Remember to praise my child for all the steps of using the toilet. Make a little basket of unique toys, books, and items to keep them seated and to help them be excited to use the potty. We can do this! Potty training is difficult, but all children eventually get the hang of it, and it's just possible that we'll all be celebrating diaper-free life before we know it.

Printed in Great Britain
by Amazon